The Love Odyssey
An Adventure in Relationship Exploration

Sabine Schoepke

The Power Life Press

The Love Odyssey: An Adventure in Relationship Exploration
Published by The Power Life Press
Redondo Beach, California, U.S.A.

SCHOEPKE, SABINE, Author
THE LOVE ODYSSEY
SABINE SCHOEPKE

Library of Congress Control Number: 2023917219

ISBN: 979-8-9891359-0-5, 979-8-9891359-1-2 paperback
ISBN: 979-8-9891359-2-9 digital

FAMILY & RELATIONSHIPS / Marriage & Long-Term Relationships
PSYCHOLOGY / Interpersonal Relations
SELF-HELP / Personal Growth / Happiness

Publishing Management: Susie Schaefer (finishthebookpublishing.com)

QUANTITY PURCHASES: Schools, companies, professional groups, clubs, and other organizations may qualify for special terms when ordering quantities of this title. For information, email contact@thepowerlifecoach.com.

Dedication

For my dear friend Merrick,
thank you for being my guiding light.

Table of Contents

Introduction

Alright, let's talk about love. We all crave it, right? That deep connection that's supposed to last a lifetime. But let's be real, despite starting out with the best intentions, the road of love isn't always a smooth ride. We get into relationships dreaming of endless moments together, but at times, we end up questioning, or even regretting, our choices.

Been there? Me too. Over two decades, I tried to keep a relationship afloat. Yet, despite my best efforts, it didn't pan out. And when I got back out there in the dating world, it seemed like happy couples were in short supply. It made me wonder if finding and keeping love was just a tall tale.

Instead of putting my head in the sand, or bitterly pointing fingers, I got curious. I started to explore love as a personal project, because, honestly, life without love feels a bit empty. It's not just about holding hands and sweet nothings; it's a fundamental part of who we are. We are not meant to do life without it.

I won't pretend to have cracked a secret code to perfect relationships. But what I've aimed for in this book is to give us all a leg up; to go a little deeper than drama talk, shed some light on what is going awry, and discuss how we can avoid some of those pitfalls. Whether you're navigating a rough patch or just feel alone, there's value in understanding our love patterns, embracing our emotions, and truly opening up.

The quest for these insights? Far from straightforward. We're all unique, with our own stories and backgrounds that influence how we connect (or disconnect). But one thing is clear: taking charge of our own growth can spark a ripple effect. Even if it's just you making changes, trust me, it's impactful.

As you flip through these pages, I invite you to walk with me on this enlightening path. It's been a rollercoaster of discoveries, moments of joy, and challenging introspections. Today, I find myself in a beautiful relationship, and the journey has spilled over, affecting how I relate to friends, family, and even colleagues. As with any type of personal growth, some people may drift away, but what remains is an enriched understanding of love and a life humming with genuine contentment.

Dive in, and let's unravel love together. By opening up my heart and leaning into authenticity, I've unearthed treasures that have truly transformed my world. The quest is worth it. Hopefully, my experiences will inspire a new chapter in your love story too.

Chapter 1

Harnessing the Power Within:
From Fear to Love in the Art of Relationships

"There is freedom waiting for you,
On the breezes of the sky,
And you ask "What if I fall?"
Oh but my darling,
What if you fly?"

— *Erin Hanson*

Imagine, for a moment, holding a brush that paints the very tapestry of your life. Each stroke, guided by your beliefs, gives shape to your reality. We're all artists, gifted with the same incredible power of creation. Yet, like any art, the masterpiece we weave depends on our technique—how deeply we feel, how vividly we imagine, and how boldly we act. Every day, as you step into the world, you embody the artwork of your personality, beliefs, and actions. The moment you recognize this, a profound realization dawns: you're not just powerful, you're transformative. And in the realm of love? Oh, the magic we can conjure there is unparalleled.

Let's get right to it: love and relationships—the most intricate dance of human connection. Much like art, they require a gentle touch, practice, and a deep understanding. But when we pause and have a look at the landscape of modern connections, it seems our brushstrokes might be a tad off. Despite our best intentions, the canvas of many relationships appears to get messed up by misunderstandings and unnecessary mistakes. It's a rather humbling reminder that, perhaps, we're still apprentices in this beautiful, complex artistry of the heart.

Remember our beginnings? Born as embodiments of pure, unfiltered love. We arrived into this world untouched by the weight of yesterday or the uncertainty of tomorrow, dwelling only in the embrace of the present. With hearts wide open, we'd express every shade of our emotions—whether they painted skies of joy or storms of distress. Fear was an unknown language; the world's opinions mere whispers against the roaring symphony of our curiosity. And if we did not like something? We'd voice it, only to swiftly return to our familiar state of wonder and playfulness.

That beautiful innate ability to love freely, to revel in the simplicity of a moment—*that* is the essence of who we once were. Think about it. Don't the memories that make our souls dance now involve laughter, creation, or the unbridled joy reminiscent of our childhood? There's a reason these moments resonate. They echo the authentic rhythms of our initial selves, reminding us of the raw, untamed love and innocence we were birthed with.

But then, the plot of our story takes a turn, doesn't it? Around the tender age of four, we begin to be molded—not just by the gentle hands of parents, but also by educators and the broader strokes of society. Instead of navigating by the compass of our innate wonder, we're handed a map with paths already drawn. It's as if our flexible minds are given to a world focused on creating the ideal software, where education sometimes feels less like enlightenment and more like coding.

The Masks We Wear: Navigating Authenticity and Adaptation

Fear, that once foreign language, becomes our tutor. We're subtly, and at times not so subtly, introduced to the shadows of punishment and the elusive promise of rewards. The innate desire to belong, to be embraced by our tribe, is overshadowed by the looming threat of rejection. Suddenly, the world's murmurs become defining choruses, shaping our actions and dreams. We don't just adapt; we transform, often trading our authentic selves for versions more palatable to the world around us.

Over time, we master the art of wearing masks. Every day, in each interaction, we put on an array of facades, tailoring our persona to fit the scene we're in. Alone, we might wear one mask (or none at all). With a partner, it morphs into another. At work, among friends, or with our children, the masks change, layering one atop the other until we can scarcely recall our original face beneath them all. It's a dance of adaptation, where the line between reality and performance starts to blur.

We don't just stretch the truth to the world; we weave tales for ourselves, stories that distance us from our genuine essence. This persistent self-deception, coupled with the tireless charade of masking, feels nothing short of a personal inferno. It's draining, and to cope with this relentless pressure to fit in, to be recognized and validated, we might find solace in substances like drugs and alcohol. We understandably turn to distractions, seeking fleeting relief from the constant fear of inadequacy, rejection, and emotional repercussions.

Today, with clarity that only hindsight can offer, I recognize my old habits for what they were: both my lifelines *and* my shackles. Whenever the weight of emotional exhaustion or fear bore down on me, I found solace in two distinct ways: alcohol and an all-consuming commitment to work.

The alcohol provided a temporary numbness, a foggy escape from the reality I didn't want to face. Each sip felt like a comforting hug, momentarily silencing the chaos in my mind. But, as the haze faded, the emptiness and pain returned, often intensified.

Immersing myself in work, on the other hand, was a double-edged sword. On one side, it made me focused, dedicated, and to the outside world, incredibly successful. Professionally and financially, this approach bore fruit. But on the other side, it was a form of escape, a way to avoid confronting the emotional turmoil within. While my professional life thrived, personally, I was running on empty. This relentless drive, though yielding external rewards, was also a self-destructive path that kept me from addressing the core issues I faced. Understanding and accepting these truths has been challenging for me. But it's the acknowledgment that set us on a path toward genuine self-awareness and ultimately healing.

Unanticipated Wounds: Life's Unexpected Turns

Even amid our best-orchestrated acts, life has a way of piercing our defenses. The world responds, often in ways we don't anticipate, and sometimes, we're left wounded and scarred. These scars, relics of past hurts, don't just fade away. They lie in wait, resurfacing when familiar scenarios play out, exacerbating our existing fears. What was once a life filled with spontaneity, love, and exploration has morphed into a frightening obstacle run of emotional landmines. The radiant canvas of our existence, once painted with vibrant hues of joy, now seems shadowed by the grays of caution and apprehension.

Introducing relationships into this intricate dance of emotions further complicates things, especially when we speak of intimate relationships, where the longing is not just for companionship but for deep, unconditional understanding. Two souls converge, each seeking the raw and unmasked version of the other. Yet, paradoxically, both remain veiled behind their self-crafted personas, nursing their emotional bruises in secret.

To truly connect with someone who wears an ever-shifting mask, who's lost touch with their true essence, and who flinches at echoes of past traumas, is undeniably daunting, to say the least. At the risk of seeming negative, let's be honest, I want to say it's almost impossible. The challenge intensifies when both parties are deeply entangled in the same web of pretense, self-disconnection, and emotional baggage. It's no surprise that such connections often falter. Honesty becomes a rarity, self-awareness a forgotten relic, and emotional eruptions become the norm rather than the exception. The result? A whirlwind of confusion and emotional chaos, and there-in lies another inferno. Moving beyond the fog of fear brings us closer to the core of love. So here comes the most pertinent question of them all... (drumroll please!):

How can we navigate this path, bridging the gap between our masked selves and our true nature, to heal the scars that obscure our essence and rediscover love?

Let's start by acknowledging the following: Often, the lens through which we view the world is not shaped by tangible events but by the emotions we harbor. These emotions are either derived from love or from fear, the two primary wellsprings of our feelings. As many are predominantly propelled by fear, our shared reality becomes a reflection of these anxieties. Surprisingly, numerous studies indicate that conventional relationships lean heavily towards fear, with a staggering 95% rooted in apprehension and a meager 5% anchored in love. It's fear that compels us to masquerade, in our desperate bid to fit in and feel cherished, and when the ghost of past traumas haunts us, it's fear that makes us recoil.

Yet, beyond this turbulent terrain of trepidation lies the realm of love. Love, in its purest form, is generous and gentle. It doesn't come with strings attached; it's driven by a genuine desire rather than obligation.

Love embodies respect and empathy, steering clear from judgment and the urge to mold others to fit our ideals. It refuses to exert control, to point fingers, or to inflict pain. Instead, love thrives on equality and collaboration, dismissing power dynamics and control.

Love fosters growth, acting as a nurturer, ensuring each individual feels complete. It doesn't breed dependency but encourages self-accountability, erasing the notion of victimhood. The energy birthed from true love fuels a kind of creativity that eclipses what one can achieve alone, weaving a tapestry more vibrant and intricate than the sum of its parts.

Recall the affirmation I started this chapter with: the inherent power within you to manifest and transform whatever your heart desires. Your beliefs shape your reality. Isn't it time we pivot from living on a default setting shaped by preconceived programs to consciously creating experiences that align with our authentic desires? Envision cultivating relationships brimming with genuine love, unbridled joy, profound freedom, and mutual respect. Harness that power that resides within you. What a beautiful thought!

On a heartfelt tangent, there was a pivotal moment for me when a realization dawned: my emotional journey wasn't a solitary trek. Understanding that I wasn't isolated in my feelings, that I *wasn't* navigating this vast emotional terrain solo, offered an immense sense of solace to me. I encourage you to pause, even if for a fleeting moment. Digest this universal truth: *You are never truly alone in this journey. You are a beautiful, complete being just as you are.* Our collective pulse beats for a singular longing — LOVE. The challenges, the emotional highs and lows, the tribulations, they resonate universally. Isn't there an undercurrent of unity in this shared journey, a warmth in this collective understanding? It's liberating, to say the least. Armed with this epiphany, let us unite our forces, hand in hand, and gracefully wade through this intricate web of love and life.

Chapter 2

The Journey of Self-Awareness:
The Cake, The Icing, and Relationships

If you've journeyed with me up to this point, grasping the nuances of why relationships often falter, then you stand at the precipice of profound transformation. You have traversed the landscape of understanding the challenges inherent to human connection. This state of recognition, of cognizance, is termed as "awareness." It's a powerful tool, a beacon of light on our path to nurturing healthier relationships.

Even better, awareness doesn't just serve as an eye-opener; it equips us with the potential to craft an alternative narrative. It hands us the paintbrush to color outside the lines we've been confined to, enabling us to foster outcomes different from our past experiences.

In understanding the role of awareness, it's crucial to recognize its dual facets:

- **Problem Awareness:** This is the initial realization, the awakening to the challenges and impediments that have been roadblocks in our relational journey. It's the ability to acknowledge the collective patterns that may have been working against our desires.
- **Self-awareness:** This goes beyond the mere identification of problems and situations. It's an introspective journey into understanding one's emotions, motivations, strengths, and vulnerabilities. It's about recognizing our unique patterns, triggers, and tendencies. By achieving self-awareness, we are better equipped to navigate our relationships, understanding not just the external factors at play, but also the internal dynamics that contribute to our interactions.

Together, these twin pillars of awareness provide a foundation on which we can rebuild our understanding of love, connection, and mutual respect. Armed with this newfound knowledge, the pathway to healthier, more fulfilling relationships unfolds before us, inviting us to venture forth with renewed hope and determination.

Embarking on the Journey of Self-Awareness

This chapter dives deep into the world of self-awareness. While the idea of a relationship usually brings forth visions of two entities intertwining, the actual dynamics are more intricate. You see, in the dance of connection, each person is accountable for their own steps. Your journey, your perceptions, your reactions – they're all yours to manage. The responsibility of the other person's actions, thoughts, or feelings does not lie with you. Hence, the spotlight of this chapter is firmly on the realm of SELF-awareness – the foundation of understanding the SELF amidst relational complexities.

One of the profound revelations you'll encounter on your journey to self-awareness is the uniqueness of personal realities. Think of it as a kaleidoscope; while the pieces inside are the same, every slight turn reveals a new pattern, a different view. Your emotions, experiences, and understanding of the world around you are strictly personal. What may be a profound truth for you might merely be a passing thought for another. This isn't to negate or trivialize anyone's experiences but to underline that realities are as diverse as fingerprints.

Despite sharing communal spaces, our emotional and cognitive worlds can be galaxies apart. Recognizing this was a watershed moment for me. Once I absorbed this fact, I inevitably began to depersonalize conflicts and misunderstandings. I started to see them not as personal attacks anymore, but as discrepancies in perception. This ''little detail'' dramatically elevated all of my relational experiences.

When two people come together, there's often a mistaken belief that they inherently understand the depths of each other's minds and souls. Yet, this presumption couldn't be any further from actuality. We each wear lenses colored by our experiences, biases, wounds, and joys. It's no wonder that actions or words that seem plain as day to one person may be utterly incomprehensible to another. The classic refrain of "How could they possibly do that?" is rooted in these distinct perceptual differences

It is also of paramount importance to grasp that these diverse realities aren't a matter of right or wrong. They're just... different. Given the spectrum of experiences and triggers each of us carries, our perception of the world around us will inevitably vary. To truly thrive in relationships, we need to not just be aware of these differences but embrace and respect them. To expect others to morph into carbon copies of our beliefs and views is not just unfair, it's unrealistic. Such desires aren't rooted in genuine connection but in control and judgment, pushing away the essence of love and making lasting love impossible.

Respecting individual realities is a cornerstone of genuine connection. It replaces judgment with understanding, control with freedom, and brings us closer to authentic love and mutual respect.

The Dangerous Path of Control

The very moment you feel the urge to mold another person to your perceptions and desires, you are unintentionally and inadvertently setting the relationship on a precarious path. This impulse often signals upcoming challenges in the relationship. It marks the onset of tension, drama, fear, and underlying power struggles that will eventually chip away at the foundation of trust and mutual respect. It's like walking on a tightrope - one misstep and everything can come crashing down.

Understanding someone's unique reality and still wanting to bend it to your own signifies a lack of genuine acceptance. This often stems from a place of insecurity or a void within ourselves. Relationships that operate on these terms become a battleground of control, with each party trying to assert their version of 'reality' over the other. This is hardly the breeding ground for love; instead, it's where love gets cruelly suffocated.

True acceptance blooms when we shed the shackles of our needs and expectations from another. It thrives when we approach relationships not from a space of want or desperation, but from a place of contentment and self-assuredness. When we are grounded in self-love, we don't approach relationships to fill our vessel or validate our worth. Instead, we view them as an opportunity for mutual growth, respect, and shared joy.

In essence, a relationship's strength isn't gauged by how much we can change someone to fit our mold but by how much space we provide for both to coexist, respecting each other's unique essence. Being secure in oneself and overflowing with self-love means that we don't approach relationships with a sense of desperation or neediness. Instead, we come into them whole, seeking not someone to complete us, but someone to complement our journey. In that space of mutual respect and understanding, love doesn't just survive; it actually thrives.

The Art of Relationship Dynamics

Imagine crafting a masterpiece in the kitchen, for example, a delicious cake. If you treat the person you're with as a pivotal ingredient, such as butter in a cake recipe, then they become indispensable. A cake without its butter is likely to be bland, perhaps dry and crumbly. Its essence is missing, and you're left with a cake that disappoints.

Consider another perspective: if you regard your partner like the frosting, their presence elevates the cake, enhancing its appearance and taste, but their absence doesn't compromise its fundamental quality. The cake remains moist, flavorful, and delicious, standing proudly on its own merits, even without the frosting.

This metaphor mirrors the dynamics of a balanced relationship. Your partner should not be something so essential that, without them, your life feels incomplete or bland. They should be like the frosting and ornate decorations on a cake, a delightful bonus that adds an extra touch of sweetness. The foundation of the cake, its basic ingredients, is symbolic of your self-worth, your passions, and your journey. It must stand firm and delightful on its own.

In the realm of relationships, the frosting and decoration represents the additional joy, comfort, and companionship a partner brings. This doesn't diminish their value; it merely places the relationship in a healthy context. The essence of partnerships should be rooted in mutual respect, genuine enjoyment of each other's company, and shared experiences that enrich life. Ideally, love should be a voluntary gift we delight in giving, rather than an obligation driven by fear, neediness, or the dread of solitude. It's about two wholesome individuals coming together, each complete in their own right, choosing to share and enhance each other's journey. Not because they need to, but simply because they want to.

Isn't it funny how life often hides lessons in the oddest places?

For me, the kitchen was a peculiar classroom. I've never been the superstar baker in my family. Quite the opposite, in fact. Everyone knew about my baking blunders. Cookies turned into runny messes that covered the entire cookie sheet. Cakes turned out overbaked and underbaked at the same time. My kids would even teasingly plead with me *not* to bake! I'd set out with the intention of making something delicious, yet despite the promising start, things would invariably go wrong. Why, you ask? I could never stick to a recipe. I'd find one that seemed alright, but instead of following it precisely, I'd start making my 'adjustments' and 'improvements'. Tweaking a bit here, substituting something there, until the end product bore no resemblance to what it should've been.

That's when it hit me. I was doing the same thing in my relationships. I'd meet someone, see the potential in them or form an image of what I wished them to be. Often, I'd overlook who they truly were, getting caught up in molding them to fit my desires. Just as with my baking, trying to tailor someone to match my whims and fancies was a recipe for disaster.

In baking *and* in love, it boils down to a balance between control and acceptance. When you find a recipe, it's been crafted by someone after many trials, much like how each person is shaped by their unique experiences. Respecting a recipe means you trust the decisions of its creator. Similarly, respecting someone means cherishing their true essence.

Twisting recipes or personalities? The results can be messy. But, when I learned to embrace both with an open heart and a willingness to appreciate their inherent uniqueness, I found joy. It's all about letting things and people be, finding harmony, or in some instances, knowing when to lovingly let go.

For the longest time, I was with someone who seemed to be constantly walking on a tightrope of insecurity. He was consumed by the fear that one day, I'd outshine him, outgrow him. The thought haunted him – what if I realized my own worth and that I didn't need him by my side? Every move of his, every word spoken, was tainted by this fear. He sought to control, to manipulate, to mold me into a version of myself that wouldn't threaten his own self-worth. Instead of cherishing our bond, he let the dread of losing me dominate our narrative.

In an ideal world, he would have celebrated my achievements and held my hand as I soared, knowing that our bond was secure. If he had been grounded in his self-worth, he'd have realized that love meant giving freedom, not taking it away. A relationship grounded in trust and mutual respect would have flourished. But instead, our journey together became a relentless game of tug-of-war, where control was the coveted prize.

The irony? I held onto us for over twenty years, in part because of my own demons, and my own fears. There was a persistent voice in the back of my head, an echo from my past, that whispered the horror of solitude, "What if you end up alone?" The idea was daunting; however, the strain of trying to mend an already fraying bond started reflecting in my health. The emotional toll was debilitating, but time, introspection, and a hefty dose of self-love taught me a painful yet liberating lesson: I couldn't fix someone else. The power to heal; to evolve, lies within each of us.

There's a distinct memory I often reflect upon, which, I believe, perfectly encapsulates the essence of what it feels like to be under constant scrutiny. Imagine you're driving a car, with your partner in the passenger seat. Instead of enjoying the journey together, every moment is punctuated by their unsolicited directives, "Speed up! You've got to make that light. Why are you going so slow? Take the next turn!" With every passing mile, their comments chip away at your confidence, joy, and enthusiasm.

Honestly, how long can you bear to drive in such a stifling atmosphere? How many journeys would you embark on before deciding you'd rather not have them in the car at all? It's evident this isn't a partnership; it's a critique in motion. This isn't about mutual trust or enjoying the journey; it's an exercise in domination, driven by their insecurities.

Awareness is our compass in such situations. It nudges us, gently at first and then more insistently, signaling that all is not well. When the weight of constant control and manipulation becomes unbearable, it's our inner awareness that helps us discern between a genuine partnership and a bond marred by one's fears and insecurities.

So then what?

When driven by an insatiable need for love and approval, we might find ourselves enduring a relationship that's far from fulfilling. We cling to the relationship, even when it's clear that the dynamic is toxic. When fear of loneliness overshadows our sense of self-worth, we allow ourselves to be controlled. We hang in there, hoping things will change, desperately seeking that elusive validation.

Here's a paradigm shift: if you're filled with genuine self-love, the idea of a codependent relationship becomes inconceivable. You become empowered, not out of arrogance, but out of a deep understanding of your own worth. You communicate your feelings assertively, drawing clear boundaries. If your partner cannot move past their need to dominate and control, your reservoir of self-love gives you the strength to walk away. It's not about seeking vengeance or being bitter; it's about recognizing that life's too short for control games and emotional warfare.

With abundant self-love, loneliness loses its grip. You realize that solitude can be more enriching than a stifling relationship. Even if that means you're on your own for a while, you're content; you have everything you need. There's a serene kind of joy in knowing that you are complete by yourself.

Think of it as baking that cake of life. When you have love – genuine self-love and love for others – you've already got the richest, most satisfying cake. Frosting? It's lovely when it's there, but your cake is already delicious without it.

Chapter 3

Embracing Wholeness:
A Journey of Self-Love, Self-Acceptance,
and The Art of Being Enough

From our previous discussion, it's evident that self-love is the bedrock of independence from external validation. It grants us the courage to voice our thoughts and desires without hesitation.

To put it simply: self-love is the most enriching bond you will ever have — the one you share with yourself. It's about embracing every facet of who you are without reservations. It's about quenching your own emotional thirst. Drawing from the cake analogy, it means savoring the cake, even if it's without the frosting.

Choosing to truly love oneself can be an uphill battle, but the victory over self-doubt is immensely rewarding. Truly loving yourself will be one of your greatest accomplishments. You know you have succeeded when you enjoy spending time alone.

In the past, the thought of solitude terrified me. There were phases in my life when I was unattached, and the very thought of heading home from work filled me with dread. I would linger in my office, long into the twilight hours. The sheer thought of returning to a house devoid of company was excruciatingly painful. My immediate remedy? A glass of whiskey, hoping it would drown the emptiness I felt; a vain attempt to bear the unbearable. There was no delight in solitude, no joy in the freedom to do as I pleased, whenever I pleased. Reflecting on that time, I can clearly see the self-inflicted inferno I was trapped in. It was a hell of my own making, filled with self-criticism, self-judgement and devoid of self-love. My own presence felt like a cruel punishment. My identity, my solo status – became a tool for self-torment. If anyone else had treated me the way I treated myself, I'd have walked away without a second thought. It's surprising how we sometimes accept from ourselves what we would never tolerate from others.

As you can see, based on my own experiences, I can vouch for how monumental a task self-love can feel, especially given the lifetime of conditioning many of us endure. This ingrained mindset often manifests as self-criticism, self-denial, and an overarching dread of rejection from those around us. If we're stuck in a belief that we fall short, it's all too easy to imagine others will see us in the same way we see ourselves. How can we possibly believe that we are deserving of others, if we don't even think highly enough of ourselves? Thus, when we find ourselves alone, these deep-seated fears amplify, whispering: "You are alone, because nobody wants you. You are not good enough. Nobody will ever want you. You will be alone for the rest of your life. You will die alone." It's a chilling sentiment, isn't it?

Surprisingly, even when we're in relationships, fear still persists. We're hesitant to truly love, haunted by the shadow of rejection. Therefore, we put on a mask, hoping that this new version of ourselves will be deemed "worthy" of love and accepted by our partner.

Looking back on my own experiences, I recognized a unique, third kind of solitude: being in a relationship yet feeling deeply isolated. My most desolate times weren't during moments of actual solitude but rather when I was beside a partner who remained emotionally and physically distant. A partner whose personal emotional wounds led him to exert control and manipulation, pushing me away in the process. That period of my life felt like a living nightmare.

Regardless of our relationship status, be it single or otherwise, fear seems to be our constant companion. Our ingrained beliefs and emotional conditioning lead us to create our own torment, irrespective of our circumstances.

Pause for a moment and truly see yourself. This introspection is vital, because only by genuinely embracing and loving who you are can you find genuine happiness and fully manifest your essence. You are uniquely you, and there's no need to masquerade as someone else. Regardless of your relationship status, you are complete and exceptional just as you are. As we know, the weight of feeling inadequate or the need to wear a mask is a heavy one to bear. Living a pretense is a path riddled with chaos and heartache. Imagine using peanut butter instead of butter in a cake, simply because you're out of butter. What a disaster! You hold the power to decide whether you dwell in self-imposed torment or embrace a more blissful existence. After all, you possess the ability to shape your reality.

True self-awareness requires an inward gaze, allowing us to deeply understand our values, passions, ambitions, thoughts, emotions, and the aspirations that shape our world. Recognizing our vulnerabilities, emotional scars, and triggers is equally vital, along with acknowledging the past burdens we carry. Remember, these burdens are uniquely yours. While you shoulder your own, your partner carries their own. It's essential to realize that each of you is accountable for addressing and managing your respective burdens; it isn't your duty to handle theirs, nor theirs to handle yours.

The ultimate goal is to embrace and cherish your authentic self, ensuring you feel whole and fulfilled independently. This allows you to engage in relationships not out of necessity for love, but from a place of wanting to share the love that overflows from within you. It's about making the deliberate choice to delight in another's company, to embark on adventures together, to spark each other's imagination, and to evolve side by side. Doesn't that sound beautiful? It's reminiscent of the carefree days of childhood when play, laughter, and discovery were at the heart of everything. Pause for a moment and immerse yourself in that sentiment. Does it evoke feelings of lightness, simplicity, amusement, and sheer joy? *That* is indeed a slice of heaven.

The next step is to embrace your partner as they are. Venture into the unknown and discover what lies ahead, just always remain true to who you are. If it feels right, continue forward. If it doesn't resonate, it's best for both to part ways. This embodies mutual respect; a valuable measure of your own wholeness. When self-love fills you, solitude isn't daunting. In fact, you relish your own company and find other avenues to spread love.

Once you grasp that everyone has their distinct emotional weight they bear, and that each of us is accountable for them, it alters how you engage. This manner of dialogue stems from genuine love and consideration for our partner, acknowledging their pains and past wounds. As we navigate this, we also find and articulate our own desires. It takes immense bravery to expose our vulnerabilities and insecurities, and place faith in one another, all the while taking ownership of our actions and the resulting consequences.

When both individuals address their own internal challenges and come together purely from a place of love, devoid of fear or obligation, what emerges is a bond unburdened by controlling tendencies, anger, jealousy, or sadness. Instead, it's enriched by mutual understanding and shared affection. In such a union, love is given freely without any expectations, and open communication fuels the relationship. This can only be achieved when one's self-love is firmly established.

How and where to find self-love?

In essence, many of our actions in life are driven by the pursuit of love. We enhance our appearances and adjust our behaviors, all in the hope of drawing affection towards us. We sometimes mask our true selves, believing that by doing so, we'll be deemed worthy of someone else's love. We extend gestures to others, hoping their appreciation translates into love. This relentless search for love often stems from our own inadequacy in loving ourselves.

Recently, I stumbled upon a TikTok video of a striking woman in tears, desperately reaching out for anyone to love her. It was a gut-wrenching scene. As tears streamed down her face, she voiced her yearning for someone — anyone — to offer her the love she so deeply craved. Her anguish and profound desire for affection resonated with me. Many of us have been in that place. Yet, we often overlook the purest form of love that exists within us. We search for validation and joy in others, without realizing that many are grappling with similar feelings of inadequacy. If they're struggling to love themselves, how can they provide the depth of love we seek? Our quest often takes us down paths leading to the wrong individuals, which amplifies our pain and distress and sets ourselves up for more pain and suffering in the future. We will never find the kind of love we need in other people, and the love we seek externally often escapes us, simply because we're searching for the wrong thing, in the wrong places.

When the love and contentment we seek reside within us, the way we relate to ourselves mirrors how we connect with others. Thus, when we engage in relationships without a desperate craving for affection, the entire dynamic changes.

Tapping into the love that resides within us is no simple task. It's an ongoing battle against the conditioning we've undergone since birth. This isn't about pointing fingers at parents or teachers; they often do their utmost given their own knowledge and circumstances. It's a confrontation against ingrained thoughts, habits, behaviors, and reflexes. A challenge against self-neglect, self-condemnation, self-rejection, self-criticism, and self-sabotage. This becomes an all-day, every-day commitment. The key lies in addressing one thought, one habit, and one behavior at a time. Avoid burdening yourself with the expectation of conquering all at once. Celebrate each moment of clarity, every decision made from love over fear. Recognize that your partner is navigating their own internal struggles and carrying their own baggage. Offer them understanding by not internalizing their actions is a win. Cherish each small triumph, for over time, they will revolutionize both your personal journey and your shared relationships.

Your self-perception shapes your reality. To truly love yourself, you need to genuinely embrace, cherish, and respect your body, mind, and spirit in their entirety. You don't require external validation, acceptance, or affection. What truly matters is your own self-assessment, acknowledgment, and love. You are radiant, flawless, and deserving of love, irrespective of external voices or internal doubts. When you become immune to your own and others' judgments and expectations, genuine love will flourish within you.

Honoring and Loving Our Bodies

In an age where social media often glorifies specific body types and aesthetic standards, it is harder than ever to accept and love our bodies unconditionally. We tend forget the incredible job our body is doing to sustain our life and health.

Deep within us, billions of microscopic cells are ceaselessly working day and night to maintain the intricate balance that keeps us healthy and vibrant. From our skin cells that provide a protective shield against external harm, to the diligent heart cells rhythmically contracting to keep blood flowing, and the brain cells transmitting lightning-fast signals for our every thought and movement; each cell plays a crucial role in our overall well-being. Each heartbeat, each breath, every movement we make, and even the thoughts we think, are results of their tireless efforts. The intricate harmony these cells orchestrate is a testament to the incredible, often overlooked, sophistication of our bodies. In this context, it becomes clear that we owe immense gratitude to these diligent, life-sustaining cells. Shouldn't we express this gratitude by treating our bodies with kindness, respect, and love? By nourishing our bodies with healthy food, engaging in regular exercise, getting ample rest, and maintaining a positive mindset? Our bodies are the vessels that enable us to experience life's many joys, and they deserve to be honored and loved.

While creating a loving attitude towards your body is a mindset exercise, I have learned over the years that just changing our thoughts to change our mindset is not enough. If we want to change our mind, we need to change our habits as well. It is the same with exercise. If you want to see real results, just working out is not going to achieve that if you are still eating crap, drinking alcohol, and not getting enough sleep. It all needs to be focused on the same goal. Here are some practical ways to love and honor your body.

Positive Self-Talk

Isn't it amazing how the words we whisper to ourselves shape the map of our hearts and souls? The conversation we hold with our inner self can carve pathways to unconditional self-love or lead us into the tangled maze of self-doubt. Instead of lingering at the crossroads of self-criticism, what if we took a moment each morning to marvel at our body's wonders? Think of it – when you wake up, you might thank your legs for carrying you through the world, your hands for their ability to create and communicate, and that unwavering heart of yours? It tirelessly ensures every inch of you thrives, pumping life's essence to and from every corner of your being.

As we embark on each day, let's start with a pledge: to serenade our beings with affirmations of gratitude, forging a bond with our bodies, one simple and cherished acknowledgment at a time. I urge you to take this next step forward and embrace this transformative practice.

Nourish Your Body

A powerful way to honor your body is through mindful eating. Rather than seeing food purely as a source of pleasure or a cause for guilt, view it as vital fuel that keeps your body running efficiently. This perspective encourages balanced and nutritious choices. For instance, savor the sweet juiciness of a ripe mango, the crunchiness of fresh carrots, or the hearty warmth of a bowl of homemade soup. Learning to appreciate the taste, texture, and nourishment that different foods provide is an act of love towards your body.

When it comes to honoring and loving your body, I encourage you to engage in mindfulness and eat in response to your body's intuition. This is not a free pass to satisfy every craving for sweets or unhealthy treats. I acknowledge that we live in an age of information overload, where clear, unambiguous information about what truly benefits our health is muddied by conflicting messages. It's further complicated by the fact that each of us is unique, with varying needs dictated by our individual health status and activity levels.

So, rather than absorbing the advice of the masses, start tuning in to your own body's signals. I've always been skeptical of entities like pharmaceutical companies or big businesses whose motives may not necessarily align with our best interests. Find a fitness or nutritional coach, or a health care provider you trust. But most importantly, trust your own body, it knows what it needs.

Regular Exercise

Physical activity is another excellent way to love and honor your body. This does not mean punishing workout routines or striving to fit an unrealistic mold. Rather, it's about engaging in activities that make you feel good and energize you. You might love the tranquility of yoga, the exhilaration of a long bike ride, or the strength you feel after a weightlifting session. The goal is to truly connect with your body and appreciate your body's abilities, improve your health, and have fun while doing it. That's why I body build, but I don't compete. For me, bodybuilding is pure bliss. It is where I am in my zone. Where my mind connects with every muscle that I work on. For me, mindfully lifting weights is a form of meditation. If you happened to observe me during my gym sessions, you'd find something perhaps a touch unusual: my eyes often remain closed as I lift. It's my way of diving deep, channeling an intimate and beautiful bond between muscle and mind. If competing were my goal, my focus would shift to meeting other people's expectations; it would get competitive, and it would get very stressful for my body. This is not my personal goal. I chose to make my personal goals my priority. And so should you.

Rest and Recovery

Just as important as physical activity, giving your body time to rest and recover is equally necessary. This might mean getting enough sleep at night, taking breaks throughout the day, or scheduling relaxation activities such as a bubble bath or a good book. By honoring your body's need for downtime, you respect its limits and support its function. I used to feel guilty about resting and enjoying myself. For me, giving myself downtime used to be a real challenge. But I have found things like napping, reading, watching my favorite tv show, and cooking that I can do guilt-free today. I celebrate myself, because I have definitely come a long way.

Mindful Dressing

The clothes you wear have a significant impact on how you feel about your body. Just like how a gorgeous dress can make us feel sexy and beautiful, so can soft and casual clothes that make us feel comfortable. Instead of trying to hide perceived flaws or squeeze into the latest trend, consider how the clothes make you feel. Find items that make you feel comfortable and confident. This approach to dressing is a celebration of your unique body and an act of self-love. When I settle into my blissful alone time, you might find me wearing an old slightly torn up sweater that my daughter once gave me and a super soft pair of sweatpants. On the other hand, I've discovered certain colors that invigorate me and imbue a sense of boldness and confidence within me. In my case, these are black, white, turquoise, and red. Your color choices are as distinct and personalized as you are; they're a deep part of who you are. Have fun exploring this side of you.

Holistic Healthcare

Honor your body by taking care of your health. Regular medical check-ups, listening to your body when it's in pain or discomfort, and seeking professional help when needed are essential parts of this process. Prioritizing your health is a testament to the value you place on your body. But remember: take on an active role when it comes to taking care of your body. Traditional healthcare can sometimes lean towards temporary fixes rather than comprehensive solutions. Be an advocate for your body.

Sexuality

As I have learned on my own journey, exploring, understanding, and embracing our own sexuality is a key part of overall wellness and self-love and ultimately the destiny of our intimate relationships. Here are some of my personal thoughts and tips from a sex-positive perspective:

Acceptance of Sexuality: We are all animals with natural, biological sexual desires. It's a normal part of life and a facet of being human. It's important to remember that as long as it's consensual and respectful, there is no right or wrong when it comes to sexuality. It is the most basic, beautiful, and natural instinct there is.

Normalize the Conversation: The more we talk about sexuality in open, respectful ways, the less shame and stigma there will be around it. This starts with self-talk, honest conversations with your partner, talking with trusted friends, or seeking professional guidance if needed.

Body Positivity: Loving your body is a journey, not a destination. It's essential to understand that everyone's body is unique and beautiful in its own way. Daily affirmations can be helpful. Regular rituals of pampering your body with oils and lotions, bubble baths, and getting massages have been part of my routine as well. My personal hack to trick myself into being nicer to myself: imagine treating your body like the body of somebody you love.

Self-Love and Exploration: Masturbation is a healthy and natural activity that is not only enjoyable but can help you understand what you enjoy. It's a beautiful form of self-care, and it allows you to become more comfortable and confident with your body and its responses. Knowing yourself and what pleasures you make an intimate relationship with somebody else even better.

Educate Yourself: There are many resources available that can help you better understand human sexuality, different types of desires, and sexual health. Books, podcasts, webinars, or professionals in the field can be good sources of information. The rule here is: the more you know, the better it gets.

Professional Help: Always remember, you are not alone. A sex therapist or counselor can provide guidance and help you navigate any challenges you might be facing regarding your sexual health or self-image. Don't stress it; address it. Sexual insecurities will not go away on their own, and they can ruin any relationship, no matter how good it is otherwise.

Consent and Boundaries: Understand and respect your boundaries and ensure that any partner you're with does the same.

Communication about what feels good, what doesn't, and what you're comfortable with is critical in any sexual relationship. Even better: be curious and playful together. The only rule is: if your partner does not respect your boundaries, they don't respect you. Get out!

Remember, everyone is on their own unique journey when it comes to body acceptance and embracing their sexuality. It's okay to take your time and to seek help when needed. There is no "normal"—there's only what feels right for YOU. I experienced sexual abuse at a very young age, so my personal journey has been a challenging one. I have healed and learned to not only accept, but truly love and enjoy my body. From my own experience, I have learned that sensuality and sexuality is a beautiful and important part of self-love.

No matter where you are right now or what your starting point is, you can enjoy enrapturing sexuality. Honoring and loving your body is a lifelong ever-evolving exploratory journey that requires mindfulness and curiosity. Really get to know your body. Treat it like the body of somebody you love. Every step you take towards positive self-talk, nourishing food, enjoyable exercise, sufficient rest, comfortable clothing, proactive healthcare, and enjoyable sexual activities is a step towards a more loving relationship with your body. Remember, it's not about achieving perfection but truly loving the unique, miraculous vessel that is your body.

Honoring and Loving Your Mind

If we choose to love and accept ourselves wholly, just like the body, our mind also deserves care, respect, and love. While the mind is our greatest curse, it is an extraordinary tool that allows us to learn, dream, create, and solve problems. I'll share with you some practical ways I found to honor and love my mind. To be honest, it's been tough at times, but I promise, it does get easier. Just give yourself some grace and remember to take it one thought, emotion, action, and reaction at a time.

I like to compare the mind to an ocean. It is vast, deep, and endlessly fascinating. It can be calm and serene or raging. Your mind is your most valuable asset, offering treasures of intellect, creativity, and empathy. But sometimes, it feels more like a tempest, filled with waves of doubt, anxiety, or negative thoughts. Here are some ideas to help you ride these waves, honoring and loving your mind in the process.

Escaping the Raging Waves

When your mind sucks you into a title wave of worry, it can feel like you're drowning. Instead of being tossed around by raging waters, try mindfulness meditation. I like using guided meditations to get back on solid and serene grounds. I have saved a few I enjoy on YouTube that are my personal go-to meditations. Simply sitting in silence and practicing observation of your thoughts without judgment, then letting them pass is another one of my favorite techniques. It's like being the calm in the center of storm, undisturbed by the chaos.

Excursions into the Unknown

The mind loves to venture into unexplored territories. Give yourself permission to satisfy this curiosity by trying new experiences or learning new things, just like children do. It's like taking your mind on a thrilling submarine ride, learning new fascinating concepts about the ocean, and encountering unusual ideas along the journey. Personally, I love to read and listen to podcasts. I also love taking cooking classes and trying different physical activities like surfing, rock climbing and fishing; things that I usually don't do or activities that expand my horizons.

The Positivity Treasure Hunt

Turn the act of positive thinking into a fun-filled treasure hunt. For every negative thought your mind generates, counteract it with three positive ones. It's like turning your mind into an archaeological site of the Titanic, digging through layers of negativity to find sparkling gems of positivity. It takes some practice to stop yourself in the midst of negative thoughts and recalibrate your mind to switch gears to positive thoughts instead. Your mind won't submit to it without putting up a fight. But remember you are the boss! Take charge of your mind!

Mental R&R

Imagine your mind as a busy beach-front in Hawaii, packed with brightly colored umbrellas and tourists. Sometimes even a fun beach scene needs some quiet hours. Make sure to give your mind regular breaks – envision sending it to a serene private island retreat. Whether it's through meditation, deep breathing exercises, or simply sitting quietly, these peaceful interludes can help rejuvenate your busy mind. I love taking regular power breaks. I recharge by sitting in the sun or going for quick walks. Afterwards, my brain feels clear and re-energized, ready to focus again. This usually gives things a different perspective.

Creativity

Just as the ocean has incredible depth with unseen layers teeming with life, creativity, possesses an immense depth. It allows us to delve into the deepest corners of our minds, uncovering unique thoughts, ideas, and solutions that were previously hidden or unexplored.

The ocean can surprise us with sudden storms or awe-inspiring marine life, just as creativity often leads to insights and ideas that seem to emerge from nowhere. These unexpected "waves" of inspiration often result in our most groundbreaking work.

Your mind thrives on creativity, just waiting to burst into action. Unleash this energy by expressing yourself. Write, paint, dance in your kitchen, cook a new recipe – let your mind play. It's like setting off fireworks in your brain, lighting up your mental sky with vibrant colors.

Growing up, I was told that activities like painting or making jewelry were a waste of time, and that those hobbies I would never amount to anything. I am a living example that this statement is just not true; however, allowing myself to explore creatively was not an easy task. I fought against my programming and it turned out that my jewelry design business gave me the lifestyle and freedom to create a life I had never imagined in my wildest dreams. I have become as successful not simply because of my creativity when it comes to jewelry design, but also because of my creativity when it comes to dreaming up business ideas and opportunities.

Calling for Backup

When the seas of your mind turn rough and stormy, don't hesitate to call for a lifeboat. Reach out to coaches or mental health professionals who can provide the support you need. It's like having a seasoned ship captain who can help you navigate through the storm and into calmer waters. I have worked with therapists and coaches most of my adult life and I would not be where I am today without the people who helped me gain new perspectives and widen my horizon. These are the people who provided me with a safe place to discover and heal parts of me that needed attention. It is challenging to mend your heart and mind using the same mindset that requires healing, but it can be done - we are just not meant to do it alone.

Honoring, loving, and nurturing your mind, even when it feels like your greatest curse, is a challenging and exciting adventure of epic proportions. It requires honesty, patience, resilience, and a sense of humor. No matter how high the waves, you have the skills and support to surf them with grace. It's all part of the magnificent journey of being human, navigating the breathtaking seascape of your mind.

Loving and honoring your mind is an ongoing and evolving process that involves mindfulness, learning, positivity, rest, creativity, and knowing when to seek help. By integrating these practices into your life, you can nurture a loving, healthy, and robust relationship with your mind, to celebrate its incredible capabilities and its indispensable role in your holistic well-being. The journey isn't about achieving a perfect state of mind, but about falling in love with your mind and treat it with the respect and love it deserves.

Honoring and Loving your Soul:
Ways to Sail the Sea Within

The vast ocean, its depth, complexity, and infinite expansiveness are mirrored in our inner beings. Inspired by the ocean analogy, let's explore some practical ways we can dive into the depths of self-love and soul-nourishment through our soul.

Recognizing the Vastness

The first step towards loving and honoring your soul is understanding its vastness. Take time each day to contemplate your inner world. For example, practice mindfulness by spending 10 minutes in silence, focusing on your thoughts, feelings, and sensations. It's like standing at the ocean's edge, witnessing the vast expanse stretching before you. By doing this regularly, you will begin to appreciate the depth and breadth of your inner self.

Embracing the Depths

Just as the ocean holds an extraordinary world beneath its surface, our soul harbors profound wisdom and untapped potential. You can explore this is through deep meditation or journaling. These practices are akin to deep-sea diving, guiding you below the surface of your conscious mind and into the depths of your soul. Don't shy away from the emotions or thoughts you may encounter; instead, let them flow naturally, observing them without judgment.

Navigating the Waves

Life, much like the ocean, is full of ebbs and flows. There will be calm days and stormy ones. To honor your soul, try adopting resilience-building strategies. For instance, when faced with a difficult situation, not unlike a stormy sea, use mindfulness techniques to remain calm and focused. Or view the situation as an opportunity for growth and learning, just as rough waves shape and polish pebbles into beautiful beach stones. It may be a tall order to remain calm when life is pulling you under, but fighting the waves is in vain; a fight you will never win. When we are taught to swim, we learn to that staying calm and using your buoyancy is a much smarter way to stay afloat. I have become much better at controlling my feelings and reactions to challenging situations. My inner dialogue now reminds me to stay calm. It nudges me to look for the silver lining and if I can't see it, it reminds me to have faith in the process; to trust that things always work out for me. I have also learned that life's pendulum swings both ways. There will be good times and not so good times. The more we resist or persist, the longer the bad times will last. Remind yourself that even the bad times will not last forever. The pendulum will always swing back the other way.

From my own journey, I've learned how challenging it can be to maintain composure during tumultuous times. Much like physical exercise, I recommend beginning with lighter challenges - the minor issues plaguing you - to cultivate the habit of calmness. This practice strengthens your resilience, so that when confronted with larger challenges, your built-up resilience aids in keeping your composure.

Protecting Your Ecosystem

Your soul thrives when you cultivate a supportive, positive environment around you, much like the myriad of lifeforms flourishing in the ocean. Surround yourself with uplifting individuals who respect and support you—these people are the vibrant coral reefs of your ecosystem. Engage in activities that you love and bring you joy, for these are the nutrients that feed your soul. You might enjoy reading, painting, or spending time in nature. Do these things just for yourself. The goal here is to enjoy. I have written dozens of poems that I have never shared with anyone; they are merely expressions of my soul. It made me so happy to let them bubble up without any judgement or expectations. This exercise does not require approval or validation from anybody, not even yourself. It just needs to make you happy.

Exploring the Unknown

Our souls, like the vast uncharted territories of the ocean, have many untapped potentials and undiscovered aspects. One approach to explore is through trying new experiences. Take up a new hobby, travel to an unfamiliar place, or learn a new language. The excitement of discovery that accompanies these ventures is comparable to an oceanographer exploring uncharted sea depths. Every time I go on a trip, I feel I discover a new part of my soul. I always give myself plenty of alone time. I go for walks, a run, or sit in silence by myself in nature. I invite my soul to share these moments with me and I listen to what comes up. It seems as though I'm gradually uncovering more about an old friend.

Loving and honoring your soul in these ways is in alignment with the ocean's beautiful metaphorical lessons. Through understanding its vastness, embracing its depths, navigating life's waves, protecting your inner ecosystem, and continuously exploring the unknown, you create a profound relationship with your soul. As you sail the sea within, you nurture the most important relationship of your life.

Coming Full Circle with Body, Mind and Soul

From my personal journey, I have learned that I am most happy, loving and accepting of myself when I create a beautiful, nurturing, and balanced home for my body, mind, and soul. I view all three aspects as "my children" for whom I keep an environment of comfort and love. I provide them with delicious, nutritious food and engage them with activities that are enjoyable, stimulating, and intriguing, while ensuring ample time for rest and rejuvenation. Their emotional, spiritual, and medical well-being is a priority for me. Furthermore, I actively engage in mindfulness, which involves attentive listening and interaction with these essential parts of my existence. Sounds like parenting, right?

The metaphor of the three-legged stool beautifully symbolizes the sacred triad of Body, Mind, and Soul. This metaphor is one of my favorite concepts and it has had a major impact on how I see my holistic wellbeing. Beloved by philosophers and spiritual teachers, it is a testament to the intrinsic harmony that weaves our existence together. The metaphor says that the key to a flourishing life, brimming with wellness and fulfillment, and therefore self-love, rests in achieving equilibrium among these three profound aspects of our being.

The essence of this metaphor lies in its striking simplicity - just as a stool stands firm and steady on three balanced legs, our lives achieve stability when body, mind, and soul are in a harmonious state of balance. If we disregard one aspect - be it our physical health, mental wellbeing, or spiritual nourishment - akin to a stool missing a leg - our life wobbles and we might fall. Thus, the true art of living and loving oneself lies in nourishing and balancing these three dimensions of our existence with mindful attention and care.

Chapter 4

Embracing Vulnerability and Communication: The Pathway to Resilient Relationships

The root cause of relationship failure, and why love often struggles to survive, lies in our pervasive misunderstanding of one another, a lack of self-love, and missing the pertinent role communication plays. To enable love to endure and prosper, we must discover and use our authentic voice, while communicating through the channels of love and respect. It's critical that we trust both ourselves and our partner, while appreciating that our partner exists in a unique reality, different from our own, burdened with their own distinct emotional baggage and that they are generally not aware of our thoughts, emotions, and needs. By recognizing this as our starting point, we set off on a more promising path.

No Conflict Communication

Couples often communicate in ways that are considered "destructive communication," which typically involves patterns of interaction that lead to misunderstandings, hurt feelings, resentment, and a breakdown of connection. All of it ultimately contributes to the slow and certain death of the relationship. Here are some most likely familiar examples of destructive communication:

Poor Listening: This includes being distracted when your partner is speaking, not giving them full attention, or often thinking of your response while they're still talking, which will lead to misunderstandings and feelings of disconnection.

Ignoring Non-Verbal Cues: Misinterpreting or neglecting non-verbal cues like facial expressions, body language, and tone will result in missing significant aspects of the message your partner is trying to convey.

Use of "You" Statements: Using "you" statements can come across as blaming or accusing. This will quickly escalate a conversation into conflict. For example, saying "You always forget to do the dishes," will certainly make your partner defensive.

Making Assumptions or Mind-Reading: Assuming you know what your partner is thinking or feeling without asking will lead to misunderstandings and create unnecessary conflict.

Lack of Empathy: Not trying to understand your partner's perspective will lead to them feeling unvalued and unheard.

Poor Emotion Regulation: Allowing emotions to escalate without taking steps to calm down can result in saying or doing things in the heat of the moment that you might later regret.

Passive-Aggressive or Aggressive Behavior: This can include anything from snide remarks to outright hostility. Such behaviors are extremely damaging to any relationship.

Stonewalling: This involves withdrawing from a conversation or conflict without resolving it. This can make the other person feel ignored or invalidated.

Criticism and Contempt: Regularly criticizing your partner or behaving with contempt (such as eye-rolling, mockery, or sarcasm) will erode the love and respect in a relationship.

Does most of this sound familiar to you? Be brutally honest with yourself. You are not alone. Unfortunately, most of us have never been trained to communicate effectively and lovingly. Communication is not just a vital part of any relationship, but it ultimately determines the destiny of every relationship we ever have. Patterns of destructive communication will create a negative cycle that is hard to break, leading to an unhealthy relationship and ultimately the death of it. Recognizing and addressing these patterns is the first step towards improving communication and strengthening the relationship.

"No conflict communication" is the opposite of "destructive communication." The concept embodies practices and techniques in communicating which can help prevent misunderstandings, resentment, and disputes between couples. It doesn't necessarily mean that disagreements won't occur – because they are a natural part of any relationship – but it's about managing and addressing those disagreements in a healthy, constructive manner. Here are several elements that define 'no conflict communication' for couples:

Active Listening: This is the act of mindful listening. Completely focusing on the speaker without interruption, to fully understand the person's feelings and views instead of preparing a counter-argument.

Understanding Non-Verbal Cues: Communication isn't just about words. Non-verbal cues such as body language, facial expressions, and tone of voice can express feelings and thoughts that words sometimes cannot. Recognizing and responding to these cues can prevent misunderstandings.

Effective Use of "I" Statements: This encourages ownership of thoughts and feelings. For instance, instead of saying, "You never listen to me," which sounds accusatory and can create conflict, try saying "I feel unheard when I talk about my day," which conveys the same message without blame.

Avoiding Assumptions and Mind-Reading: It's important not to assume what your partner is thinking or feeling. Instead, encourage open and honest communication. Ask open-ended questions to get a better understanding of your partner's perspective.

Fostering Empathy: This involves putting yourself in your partner's shoes and attempting to understand their perspective. This can reduce the likelihood of conflict and increase mutual understanding.

Recognizing and Regulating Emotions: This means identifying when you're becoming emotionally charged and possibly taking a break from the discussion until you're in a calmer state. It's easier to have a productive conversation when emotions are stable.

Proactive and Regular Check-ins: Rather than waiting for conflict to arise, proactive communication involves checking in with each other regularly about feelings, experiences, or any potential areas of concern. This can help address issues before they escalate.

Implementing 'no conflict communication' does not mean a relationship will be devoid of conflict. It aims to ensure that when disagreements do occur, they can be navigated in a manner that promotes understanding, respect, and resolution, rather than damage and discord.

Having delved into the process of self-discovery, acknowledging our individual roles and responsibilities as partners, and recognizing the intrinsic origin of our love needs, we have laid a strong foundation for our journey. We have also shed light on communication styles that cultivate and amplify love in a relationship. With this knowledge, let's transition into exploring the practical application of enlightened communication, paving the road towards a deeper, more enriching bond.

My Yummy Communication Recipe:
1. Own your individual needs.
2. Request what you desire without accusatory tones.

Embracing this method has brought a sense of equilibrium to my personal journey. While I find solace in addressing and owning my needs, it's equally rewarding to express myself with grace. Not only does this provide clarity for me, it also offers my partner a glimpse into my reality and perspectives, fostering deeper understanding between us. (It's crucial to remember that we each navigate our own unique realities, right?) In the throes of genuine love, a partner naturally yearns to bring happiness to the other. A clearer understanding of your needs can only make this task easier, something they're likely to appreciate. With this, giving and receiving becomes a heartfelt act, not a response to conflict or pressure. This transforms you from codependent individuals to co-creators, to establish a partnership thriving on mutual creation and growth.

I would phrase my ''requests'' as follows. Here is an example: "I would like to ask you for something. I know you think of me often. Because both of my kids just went off to college, I sometimes feel a bit lonely and sad. Would you mind calling me a little more often right now? It would make me really happy to hear your voice." I am aware of my needs and I communicate it in a loving non-accusatory way. This is an actual real-life example and my partner's response was very sweet. He smiled, hugged me, and after giving me a kiss, he said "Of course, babe. I would love to make you happy. Thank you for letting me know. I had no idea...you always seem so strong to me."

It's a simple and easy formula. I am aware that the approach of open, honest communication, and owning individual needs comes with its own set of risks, most often among them being vulnerability. Let's not sugar-coat it. Being prepared for what might potentially happen will make things easier to deal with:

Risk of Rejection or Dismissal

Expressing your needs and desires can make you feel exposed. There's always a risk that your partner may not understand, might dismiss your feelings, or could react negatively.

The risk of rejection or dismissal, while daunting, does offer a valuable opportunity for reflection and evaluation of the relationship's health.

When expressing our needs and emotions, we open up a channel for our partners to better understand us. However, if a partner repeatedly rejects or dismisses these feelings, it can serve as a key indicator of potential disconnect in the relationship. This continual pattern of dismissal may signify a lack of empathy, understanding, or unwillingness to accommodate your emotional needs, which are fundamental components of a healthy, loving relationship.

If such behavior persists, it might be worth considering whether this relationship aligns with your needs and well-being. A loving partner should not consistently invalidate your feelings or dismiss your needs. Instead, they would listen, empathize, strive to understand, and fulfill your needs to the best of their ability, as love tends to evoke a natural desire to see the other person happy and content.

It's important to remember that everyone has moments of misunderstanding or failure to meet the other's needs perfectly; we're all human. However, if dismissive behavior is a persistent pattern, it's a valid reason to question the relationship's dynamic.

In the face of such adversity, it's crucial to maintain open communication. Discussing concerns with your partner might lead to improvements, as they may not be fully aware of their actions. If the situation doesn't improve despite your efforts, it may be time to re-evaluate the relationship or possibly seek professional guidance, such as couples counseling.

While the risk of rejection or dismissal can be emotionally challenging, it can also be a tool for assessing the quality of your relationship and ensuring that it's one of mutual respect, understanding, and love.

Risk of Misunderstanding

Despite our best efforts, our messages may not always be received as intended. Your partner might misinterpret your expressions of need as demands or criticisms, potentially causing conflict.

Misunderstandings can lead to conflict, so managing and preventing them is essential for healthy communication. In cases where your expression of needs is misunderstood, here are several steps you could consider:

Clarify Intentions: Start by clarifying your intentions behind expressing your needs. Ensure your partner understands that your intent is not to criticize or demand, but to share your feelings and needs for a happier, more harmonious relationship.

Use "I" Statements: When communicating your feelings, the use of "I" statements can reduce defensiveness and foster understanding. Instead of saying, "You make me feel ignored," try saying, "I feel ignored when I'm speaking and you're looking at your phone."

Ask for Feedback: Encourage your partner to share how they've interpreted what you've said. This gives you a chance to rectify any misconceptions or misunderstandings immediately.

Rephrase Your Message: If your initial explanation was not clear, try to rephrase your message. Using different words or examples can help to convey your point more effectively.

Practice Active Listening: When your partner is explaining their understanding or their reaction to your words, listen actively. Show genuine interest and patience in understanding their perspective.

Express Empathy: Try to empathize with how your partner might be feeling. If they've misunderstood you, they might feel confused, accused, or overwhelmed. Acknowledging their feelings can help them to feel understood and open up to understanding your perspective better.

Seek Professional Guidance: If misunderstandings continue to occur, it may be useful to involve a neutral third party, such as a relationship counselor, who can help facilitate clearer communication. It can be challenging to communicate in a way that is effective and makes sense for your partner.

Remember that the goal is not to win an argument but to achieve mutual understanding and respect for each other's needs and feelings. Effective communication is an ongoing process that requires practice, patience, and effort from both parties involved.

Risk of Unreciprocated Vulnerability

The risk of unreciprocated vulnerability involves opening up emotionally and revealing your deepest feelings, needs, or fears, only to find that your partner does not respond in a kind way or fails to acknowledge your openness adequately. This lack of reciprocity can lead to feelings of imbalance, exposure, or emotional isolation. Here's a deeper look at what unreciprocated vulnerability might look like:

One-sided Openness: You frequently share your thoughts, feelings, and concerns, but your partner does not reciprocate or minimizes the significance of your disclosures.

Lack of Empathic Response: Your partner doesn't demonstrate empathy or understanding when you share your vulnerabilities.

Emotional Disconnection: Over time, you may start to feel emotionally distant from your partner due to the lack of mutual vulnerability.

Increased Fear and Anxiety: The ongoing lack of reciprocation can lead to increased fear of vulnerability, anxiety about sharing your feelings, or doubts about the relationship.

What are your options when faced with unreciprocated vulnerability?

Express Your Feelings: Start by openly discussing how you feel with your partner. They might not be aware of their lack of reciprocal vulnerability or understand how it affects you.

Encourage Their Openness: Sometimes, a person may struggle to open up due to past experiences, fear of vulnerability, or lack of communication skills. Encourage your partner to express their thoughts and feelings and reassure them that it's safe to do so in the context of your relationship.

Patience and Understanding: Remember that becoming comfortable with vulnerability often takes time. Your partner may need time and space to feel safe and confident in expressing their feelings or needs.

Seek Professional Help: If the lack of reciprocal vulnerability continues, it may be beneficial to seek help from a relationship counselor or therapist. They can provide strategies and exercises to encourage open and mutual vulnerability.

Reevaluation: If, despite your best efforts, your partner continues to resist sharing vulnerability, it may be worth considering the overall health and future of the relationship. Reciprocal vulnerability is key to deep emotional intimacy, and its continued absence may lead to long-term relationship dissatisfaction.

Remember, it's important to maintain a balance between expressing your needs for reciprocal vulnerability and respecting your partner's comfort and pace with opening up to you. Every individual is unique in their ability and readiness to be vulnerable, and patience often plays a crucial role in this process.

Despite these risks, the benefits of such an approach usually far outweigh the potential pitfalls. Making ourselves vulnerable is a vital part of deepening intimacy in a relationship. Here's why:

Fosters Trust: Being open and honest about your feelings and needs can build trust. It shows your partner that you're willing to take risks for the sake of the relationship.

Increases Connection: When you share your inner world with your partner, it can help them to understand you better. This can lead to a stronger emotional connection.

Promotes Growth: Vulnerability can lead to personal growth and a better understanding of oneself. It also encourages your partner to do the same, contributing to mutual growth within the relationship.

Enhances Communication: The more comfortable you become with expressing your feelings and needs, the more effective your communication can become. This can help to prevent conflicts and misunderstandings.

Deepens Intimacy: Vulnerability allows for the deepening of emotional intimacy, as you and your partner will be sharing parts of yourselves that you might normally keep hidden.

While there are risks in making ourselves vulnerable and openly communicating our needs, the potential rewards make it a worthwhile endeavor. It's an essential step in the journey toward a deeper, more fulfilling relationship and staying true to what it is that we are seeking for ourselves in a relationship.

Don't Stress It (or ignore it). Address It.

Addressing issues head-on is an absolute must in any relationship, but in intimate relationships especially. Shoving your problems under the rug or letting them simmer on the back burner is a surefire way to kill the love and energy in your relationship.

Ignoring problems is like throwing a ticking time bomb in your emotional closet. Over time, you are stacking resentment on top of resentment. And guess what? It's not a question of *if* it will blow up, but *when*. This emotional time bomb will debilitate your communication, fill your life with negativity, and drive a wedge between you and your partner.

One of the things I consistently talk about with clients, as well as friends and family, is satisfaction - in your work, in your personal growth, and in your relationships. I like to compare an unresolved issue to a stone in your shoe. At first, it's just uncomfortable, but the longer you ignore it, the more painful it becomes until it's all you can focus on. You can't enjoy the journey if you're constantly wincing in pain, can you?

Here's something else you might not realize - bottling up your emotions and unresolved problems isn't just bad for your relationship. It's bad for you, too. That stress? It's like poison for your mind *and* your body. I spent years in a dysfunctional relationship and it was making me physically ill, experiencing digestive issues and constantly sick, one illness after another. Ever since I left the relationship, about seven years ago, I have not had a single head cold and all of my digestive issues miraculously disappeared.

Keep It the Team

Another common practice is to talk (or vent) to your friends or family about your relationship issues. Here's the thing - you're not dating your friends and family; however, you *are* building a life with your partner. Every time you share your intimate problems with someone else, you're eroding the trust and privacy that's supposed to be sacred in your relationship.

Significant downsides of sharing your relationship issues with friends or family is the unintended consequence of emotionally reliving the problem. Every time you bring up the issue, it's like replaying a bad movie scene. Not only are you keeping the problem alive in your mind, you're reinforcing the negative emotions associated with it.

Your body doesn't differentiate between experiencing the problem for the first time and rehashing it over and over again. This means each time you review and repeat the story, your body is releasing the same stress hormones as if you're in the midst of the conflict again. It's like picking at a wound instead of letting it heal. It also correlates that the constant loop of stress and negative emotion doesn't just amplify the issue in your mind, it takes a toll on your physical health as well.

And to make things worse: while you're busy repeating your issues, you're missing out on the chance to create new, positive experiences, like constantly running on a treadmill of negativity without moving forward.

At the end of the day, the solution isn't to rehearse your problems with others; it's to face them head-on with your partner. Communicate openly, resolve the issues at hand, and then leave them in the past where they belong. Let's face it, your loved ones mean well, but they're looking at your relationship through their own lens.

Their advice (whether you've asked for it or not) is colored by their experiences, their biases, their fears, and their dreams.

Look at your relationship in the following dynamic - your partner is your teammate. That's it. A teammate, not your enemy. Your mission is to learn how to tackle the issues together, not just for the sake of resolving conflicts, but for building a deeper, more authentic connection. If you really find yourself in a tight spot, there's no shame in seeking professional help. Just leave others out of it.

If the relationship is worth it, the goal is not to avoid conflict but to learn how to navigate through the conflict together and see it as an opportunity for positive growth. That's what brings you closer; that's what keeps love strong. And *that's* what this darn book is all about.

The Unseen Iceberg: Ignoring Issues, Drifting Apart, and the Illusion of Greener Grass

Let's dive into a topic that's real and raw - the danger of sweeping issues under the rug in a relationship. You might think you're keeping the peace, but you're setting yourself up for a loveless, resentment-filled journey. Ignored issues are like silent termites, eating away at the core of your relationship - your love, respect, and emotional connection.

Here's what happens next. You meet someone new, and this person hits all those sweet spots that seem to have gone cold in your current relationship. You start getting distracted, pulling away from your partner, and before you know it, you're wrapped up in the intoxicating whirlwind of a new affair.

It's easy to mistake the thrill of novelty for real, substantial improvement. When you're knee-deep in dissatisfaction, every blade of grass on the other side seems greener. But remember, all that glitters is not gold. That new relationship? It's just not weathered enough yet. You're seeing the sunshine without having weathered the storm.

An affair is often the point of no return for most relationships. It's like throwing a grenade into what could've been a garden in full bloom, if only you had watered it with love, attention, and open communication.

We forget that relationships are not about finding the perfect person, but about loving an imperfect person perfectly. If you would have nurtured your original relationship, focusing on understanding yourself, practicing self-love, and communicating your needs clearly and honestly, you might've watched it blossom into something truly beautiful.

Yet, here you are, starting over in a new relationship, and the cycle continues. Unless you learn from the past, you're destined to repeat the same patterns and mistakes. The key isn't finding a new partner; it's becoming a better partner yourself.

So, let's get real about our relationships. Keep the communication channels open. Tackle the issues as they come. Decide whether or not the relationship is right for you, and if so, pour love into your relationship and watch it grow. In the end, true love isn't about constantly seeking something new; it's about making something old new again, every single day.

In a Nutshell

As we arrive at the end of this exploration into the world of relationships, lasting love, and personal growth, I am truly grateful for the journey we have embarked upon together. From my own life lessons to the insights gleaned through the stories of others, we've ventured into the complex landscape of human interactions, explored the intricacies of love and emotional intimacy, and discovered invaluable strategies to nurture relationships that thrive on self-love, understanding, compassion, and authenticity.

Our journey together through the pages of this book hasn't been about finding the perfect formula for relationships, because no such formula exists. Relationships, like human beings, are dynamic and complex, and they often reflect the idiosyncrasies of our individual selves. They demand our time, our attention, our love, and our commitment to grow.

Yet, what we have done, what we have achieved, is profound. We learned to approach relationships with fresh eyes, embracing the ebbs and flows, and developing the resilience to weather the storms. We learned the importance of authenticity, of daring to reveal our true selves and allowing others to do the same. We discovered that compassion is not just a feel-good concept, but a practice that can bridge the widest of gaps and mend the deepest of wounds. And most importantly, we've come to recognize that the journey towards love begins with an inward journey, one of self-discovery, personal growth, and ultimately self-love.

I encourage you, as we part ways, not to see this as the end of our shared journey. Rather, consider it the launching pad for your own ongoing exploration, for a life of continuous growth, love, and relationships that reflect the best in you. Just because you deserve it. Embrace the chance to redefine your relationships, whether romantic, familial, or platonic. Use these principles as stepping stones towards an existence that thrives on deep, authentic, and lasting connections. Apply the lessons you've learned here not just to the relationships you have, but also to the ones you are yet to create, to the person you are and the person you are becoming.

Seven years ago, when I stepped back into the world of dating, I was filled with despair. But as I stand here today, with a love that continues to deepen and a life enriched by relationships that bring me joy, I can attest to the transformative power of self-awareness, open communication, and an unyielding commitment to personal growth and self-love.

To you, my dear reader, I offer my deepest gratitude. Your willingness to accompany me on this journey, your courage to confront the unexplored territories of your own heart, and your determination to seek lasting love and happiness, are truly inspiring.

Take these lessons with you as you move forward. Let the principles you've learned guide you, whether you're currently nestled in the warmth of a loving relationship, battling the turmoil of a troubled one, or braving the world of dating once again.

In the end, this journey we've undertaken is not just about building stronger relationships; it's about becoming better versions of ourselves. It's about inviting love into our lives and letting it flourish—not merely in our relationships, but in our very being. It's about living in a state of continuous love, not only for others but for ourselves.

Step into this new chapter of your life, and remember: the goal isn't to find love, but to embody it, to become a beacon of love that illuminates every corner of your existence; just like in John Mayer's song "Love Is a Verb." In doing so, you will create not just happier relationships, but a happier, more fulfilling life for yourself and all the people you touch.

Here's to our shared journey, to the lessons learned, the growth achieved, and to the love that awaits us all. The world may seem daunting, but let us remember that with love, resilience, and commitment, we can transform our relationships, our lives, and ultimately ourselves.

Thank you for joining me on this journey. Now, let the adventure continue. Embrace love, embrace growth, embrace the extraordinary potential that lies within you. Because you, my dear reader, are not just deserving of love. You are love, waiting to happen.

Acknowledgments

First, a nod of gratitude to the one I've often overlooked – me. I seldom pause to commend myself, so here's to the bravery of stepping back into the dating world and committing to a journey of authenticity. High-fives to myself for resilience in navigating those not-so-great moments.

To those who unwittingly became subjects of my study – the commendable, the challenging, and those who gave 'nightmare date' a new definition, thank you. Each one, in their unique way, enriched the tapestry of this project.

A massive shoutout to my anchors, Sebastian and Allie. Navigating dating with kids isn't a cakewalk, and you sweetened those moments of angst with love, giggles, listening to me rant, and timely ice cream interventions.

Merrick, my guiding star and unwavering mentor, you've left an indelible mark on my life, pushing me to realms I would have never ventured into. Every word in this book owes its genesis to you. Even when our coffee dates are a rare event, your place in my heart is permanent.

Roderick, my inadvertent relationship guinea pig – this book is, in many ways, our shared story. Every lesson here was a shared experience at some point in our journey.

To the dynamo that is Susie from Finish the Book Publishing – you've been more than a guiding hand in this journey. Beyond your expertise, it's your luminous spirit that I'm so grateful for. Here's to coffee dates in European cafes and many more collaborations!

Lastly, to you, my cherished reader. Your engagement breathes life into my work. May this book be a ray of hope, a source of smiles, and a guide in your quest for love. Never let the flame of faith in love dwindle.

About the Author

A writer, podcaster, life coach, speaker, philanthropic serial entrepreneur, and mom to twins, Sabine Schoepke has consistently been drawn to life's trials, facing them head-on. Deeply intrigued by emotional intelligence, Sabine's innate gift lies in unearthing the positive amidst adversity, using her gifts to channel insights to guide others in unlocking their true potential in relationships, personal, and professional growth.

Discover more about Sabine's transformative journey and her mission at ThePowerLifeCoach.com. You can become a part of her vibrant Radical Mindset Transformation Technology community at ThePowerLifeCoach.com/RMTT.

https://www.facebook.com/
SabinePowerLife

@sabine_power_life

https://www.linkedin.com/in/
sabineschoepke

https://www.youtube.com/
@sabine_power_life

@sabine_power_life4ever